W9-DEL-093

Bee and Flea Go to the Sea

Mary Elizabeth Salzmann

Consulting Editor, Diane Craig, M.A./Reading Specialist

Published by ABDO Publishing Company, 4940 Viking Drive, Edina, Minnesota 55435.

Printed in the United States.

Credits
Edited by: Pam Price
Curriculum Coordinator: Nancy Tuminelly
Cover and Interior Design and Production: Mighty Media
Photo and Illustration Credits: BananaStock Ltd., Brand X Pictures, Comstock, Corel, Digital Vision, Eyewire Images, Hemera, ImageState, Tracy Kompelien, PhotoDisc, Stockbyte

Library of Congress Cataloging-in-Publication Data

Salzmann, Mary Elizabeth, 1968-
Bee and flea go to the sea / Mary Elizabeth Salzmann.
p. cm. -- (Rhyme time)
Includes index.
ISBN 1-59197-776-2 (hardcover)
ISBN 1-59197-882-3 (paperback)
1. English language--Rhyme--Juvenile literature. I. Title. II. Rhyme time (ABDO Publishing Company)

PE1517.S35 2004
428.1'3--dc22

2004050799

SandCastle™ books are created by a professional team of educators, reading specialists, and content developers around five essential components that include phonemic awareness, phonics, vocabulary, text comprehension, and fluency. All books are written, reviewed, and leveled for guided reading, early intervention reading, and Accelerated Reader® programs and designed for use in shared, guided, and independent reading and writing activities to support a balanced approach to literacy instruction.

Let Us Know

After reading the book, SandCastle would like you to tell us your stories about reading. What is your favorite page? Was there something hard that you needed help with? Share the ups and downs of learning to read. We want to hear from you! To get posted on the ABDO Publishing Company Web site, send us e-mail at:

sandcastle@abdopub.com

SandCastle Level: Transitional

Words that rhyme do not have to be spelled the same. These words rhyme with each other:

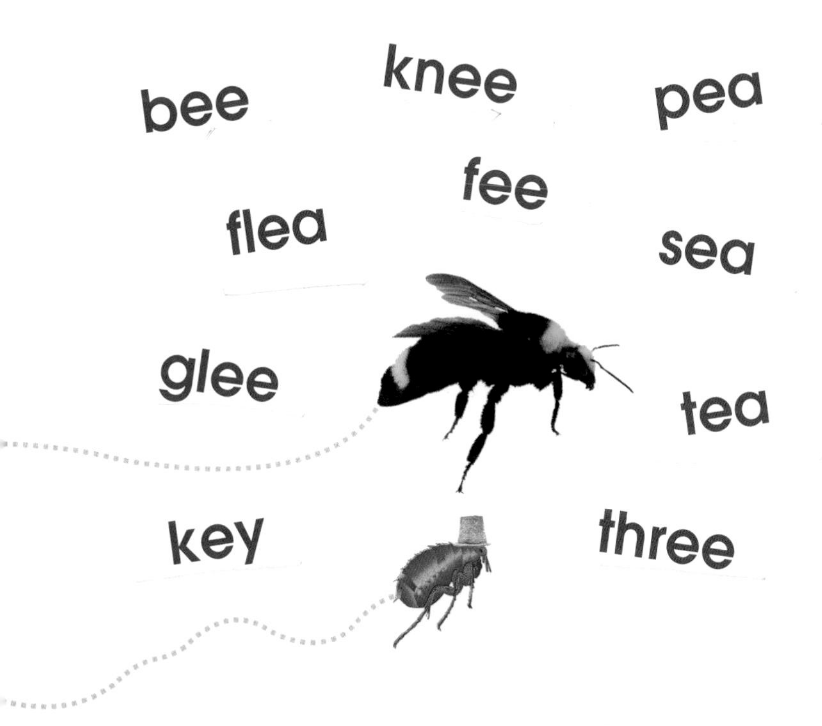

Davy and Ivan give Wags a bath to get rid of every last **flea**.

Elise is a ballerina for Halloween.

Her brothers are a lion and
a **bee**.

Ben wears his house **key** on a string around his neck.

After his checkup, Elliot's mom will pay the doctor's **fee**.

Felicia likes carrots and zucchini but won't eat even one **pea**.

When he rides on his dad's shoulders, Alex laughs with **glee**.

Hector's family takes a vacation by the **sea**.

Michael sits on his dad's knee.

Veronica, Sandy, and Robin are having tea.

Heidi has three peas on her fork.

Bee and Flea Go to the Sea

Bee and Flea leave at three.
They are taking a trip to the sea.

On the way to the sea, Bee finds a key.
The key opens a door in a tree.

Inside the tree,
Bee and Flea
find a golden pea.
Flea giggles with glee!

Bee says, “We can use the golden pea to buy tea when we get to the sea!”
“Great idea!” says Flea, because tea isn’t free.

Bee and Flea
arrive at the sea.

They order some tea
and use the golden pea
to pay the fee.

Flea sits on Bee's knee.

Flea and Bee drink their tea by the sea.

Rhyming Riddle

What do you call
the price to swim in the ocean?

Sea fee

Glossary

checkup. a routine examination by a doctor

fee. an amount charged for a service

flea. a tiny, wingless insect that feeds on the blood of animals and people

glee. joy or delight

zucchini. a long, thin summer squash with dark green, smooth skin

About SandCastle™

A professional team of educators, reading specialists, and content developers created the SandCastle™ series to support young readers as they develop reading skills and strategies and increase their general knowledge. The SandCastle™ series has four levels that correspond to early literacy development in young children. The levels are provided to help teachers and parents select the appropriate books for young readers.

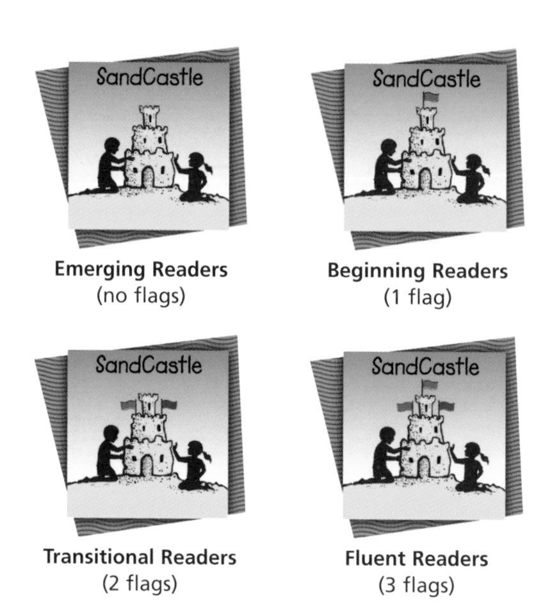

Emerging Readers
(no flags)

Beginning Readers
(1 flag)

Transitional Readers
(2 flags)

Fluent Readers
(3 flags)

These levels are meant only as a guide. All levels are subject to change.

To see a complete list of SandCastle™ books and other nonfiction titles from ABDO Publishing Company, visit **www.abdopub.com** or contact us at:

4940 Viking Drive, Edina, Minnesota 55435 • 1-800-800-1312 • fax: 1-952-831-1632